Management

41 Management Tips to Improve Your Small Business

DAVID A. HILTON, DBA

© 2018 Strategic Vision Business Development Corp. All rights reserved.

All rights reserved. No portion of this book may be reproduced in any form without permission from the publisher, except as permitted by U.S. copyright law.

CONTENTS

Introduction   vii

It's More Than a Paycheck: How to Get Your
    Team to Trust You   1
Are You Hiring for the Right Reasons?   3
Your First Hire Can Make or Break Your Business   6
5 Ways to Boost Teamwork in Your Workplace   9
Business Management Secrets: Build a Winning Team   12
Build a Winning Team: Set the Standards   14
Build a Winning Team: Put Your People in
    Position to Succeed   16
Build a Winning Team: Develop Your Workforce   18
Build a Winning Team: Four Steps for More
    Effective Teams   20
Choose the Right Guy or Gal: What to Look for
    When Hiring a Leader   23
Are Your Employees Fulfilled? (And Why
    it Matters!)   26
How to Manage Projects More Effectively:
    Three Steps   29
What Can You Do When Tough Feedback
    Upsets An Employee?   32
Employee Evaluations Can be Extremely
    Valuable… Are Yours?   35
Four Ways to Reduce Employee Turnover   37

Three Ways to Keep Your Employees Engaged	40
Small, Focused Teams can Accomplish Big Things	43
Stop Making Life Difficult… Start Making More Money!	46
Build Stronger Teams: Three Steps for Maximum Effectiveness	49
5 Ways to Derail Your Employee Empowerment Plans	52
It's NOT All About the Money: The Truth About Motivation	55
Want to Boost Employee Performance? Get Out of Their Way!	57
Boosting Employee Performance	60
What Can The NFL Teach You About Your Business?	63
When is it Time to Cut Ties with an Employee?	66
Honesty is the Best Policy, so Make it Part of Your Company Culture	69
World Class Employee Engagement the Ritz Carlton Way	71
You Shouldn't Have to, but You Must: How to Deal With Employees Who Dress Poorly (or Worse!)	74
Don't Let Skeptical Employees Sabotage Innovation in Your Workplace	77
Cut the Crap Already! (Why You Should Stop Accepting Excuses)	80
Delegation and Follow-Up: Will The Job Get Done?	83
Do You Have a "People Plan"?	86

Management Secrets: Maximize Employee Productivity	89
Management Secrets: How to Build Effective Teams	92
Management Secrets: How to Keep Your Employees Motivated	95
Leaving Your Company in Good Hands: Traits of Great Managers	98
Three Ways to Demoralize Your Employees and Make Them Less Effective	101
Small Business Management Secrets: Keep it Fresh!	104
Do Your Business Teams Deliver Reports… or Results?	107
Improve Your Hiring Process by Asking the Right Questions	110
Do You Seek Agreement… or Consensus?	113
Bonus Tip - The Ultimate Purpose of Management	116
Meet David Hilton	123

INTRODUCTION

I have read well over a hundred books on business. Sometimes it never seems as though the solutions to business are simple. Heck, it is why my clients often hire me, they need a consultant to help guide them through some of the rigors of business.

Sometimes I am hired to take a business to the next level, but other times I am hired to assist with more dire situations. However, most of the time, a lot of the issues businesses face are remarkable similar.

Management in particular seems to be where many small businesses struggle. So many new entrepreneurs start their business and run it fine and well on their own, but as that business begins to expand, the management starts to overwhelm them.

They are desperate to continue running their business, but can recognize that they themselves and possibly their business are struggling. But often overlook the cause of this struggle, management mistakes often contribute substantially.

But given their willingness to hire me, or in your case reading this book, it does show a commitment to success which is the first step to improving their management plan and skills.

Since you have made this commitment, this book is intended to share with you a few strategies to improving your ability to manage and perhaps offer a few tips that you might not have considered and develop a company you envision. With your commitment to your success and the success of your business, these tips will help you develop your business.

So long as you keep an open mind and are willing to reflect on yourself and your business so that you can identify for yourself what may need to be changed and try to see which tips can be applied to your overall management strategy. This book won't give you all the answers, but it should give you some and hopefully give you the insight you need to start to improve your business.

I hope for your success and believe this book will help contribute to that.

IT'S MORE THAN A PAYCHECK: HOW TO GET YOUR TEAM TO TRUST YOU

One of the most overlooked questions when it comes to leadership is very simple: does your team trust you?

I know what many of you are thinking: "It doesn't matter if they trust me personally or as a leader… as long I sign their paychecks, they'll perform!"

But there is a big difference between an employee doing just *enough* to get by, and an employee who dedicates himself to excellence day in and day out.

Getting the best out of your employees requires more than just a fat paycheck. It requires trust.

When your employees trust that you will make the right decisions, they are more willing to invest themselves their work, because they know that they aren't just spinning their wheels. When your employees trust that you are looking out for their best interests, they are willing to go above and beyond the call of duty when you ask them to.

So how can you inspire their trust? Below are three ideas.

1. **Listen to their ideas and ask for feedback.** Unless your goal is to create a team of mindless robots who can follow directions but can't think for themselves, you need to *listen* to your team. Don't be dismissive of their ideas and their feedback, even if they are off the mark. Ask for input regularly.
2. **Don't make emotional decisions.** It's frustrating for your employees to spend time and energy on a given project, only to have the direction changed or the project cancelled altogether. Don't change your mind on a dime. Don't overreact to a crisis. Don't speak without thinking first. Show your employees that you value their hard work and their dedication by not making emotional decisions on a whim.
3. **Learn to apologize.** A good leader must develop the ability to *apologize* when necessary. I know that this isn't easy. Whether it is losing your temper with an employee, mistreating a customer, or making a poor decision as a manager, apologizing to your team proves that you hold yourself to the same standard as you hold them to. And it shows that you value your team as *people*, not just employees.

You can't get the most out of your employees unless they trust you. So get busy earning their trust!

ARE YOU HIRING FOR THE RIGHT REASONS?

Hiring employees is a big deal, and it's very exciting for most business owners.

Business owners who don't have any employees cannot wait until the day they can make their first hire. Business owners who employ a small workforce can't wait until the day that they can make their next hire.

Growing your business is great! Hiring new employees is great! But, over the years, I've discovered that many business owners are letting their excitement cloud their judgment, and they wind up *hiring for the wrong reasons.*

Take a few moments to answer these questions honestly. Why do you want to hire employees? Is it because:

- You want to appear successful?
- You want to impress your friends or family?
- You're busy, and you don't want to work as hard?

- You want to help out a friend by hiring them?
- Or is because you have identified specific positions that, once filled by the right person, will allow your business to grow?

As you probably can guess, only the last reason on the above list is an acceptable reason to make a new hire. A large workforce may impress your friends and make you look successful—but you won't impress anyone when you are forced to shut down because your payroll is too high. Hiring an employee to reduce your workload isn't a bad idea, but if you haven't identified specific roles and responsibilities for your new employee, it won't work. And as you may know from experience, hiring someone solely as a personal favor is always a mistake. You're in business to make money!

Take some time to think about your hiring plan. Have you created an organizational chart, documenting the positions you hope to fill as your business grows? Have you specified the roles and responsibilities that each position will be responsible for? Don't worry if you haven't, few business have done this. But it's time to get busy, because if you don't have a strategic hiring plan, you are going to end up hiring employees for all of the wrong reasons. Rather than growing your business, you will find that your workforce is a weight pulling it down.

So why do you want to hire? Do you have a specific plan, and a specific purpose behind each hire you are planning to make? Don't fall victim to the same mistakes that many of your competitors are making—when you do make a hire, make sure you are doing so for the right reasons!

YOUR FIRST HIRE CAN MAKE OR BREAK YOUR BUSINESS

Most businesses start as a one-man show. And typically, a business continues that way for quite some time, until the owner becomes so overwhelmed with work that he or she is forced to hire help. (Sound familiar?) And while hiring that first employee is a *great* step to take, as it allows you to begin to truly grow your business, if the first hire isn't handled correctly it can be a disaster. Trust me – I've seen it time and time again, and I'd be glad to share some "horror stories" if you want to hear them!

The first employee that you hire will have a tremendous impact on the future of your business, and there are many factors that you must think about before making the hire. Unfortunately, this process is often rushed, because the business owner is so overwhelmed that he doesn't take the time to think it through. Resist the temptation to rush. Below are several steps that *must* be taken before making that first hire.

1. **You must clearly define the role you are hiring for.** It sounds obvious, but many business owners don't do this, instead, they hire an employee for a vaguely defined role and let the chips fall as they may. Before making a hire, you need to decide exactly what your new employee's role will be. Sales? Accounting? Shipping? A combination of roles? There is no right or wrong answer here… as long as there is a clearly defined role.
2. **Find an employee that complements your skill set.** It is human nature to hire someone that you get along with. And it is important that you get along with your new employee, but it is more important that their skills complement yours. If your gift is sales, don't hire another salesperson. Find someone that can handle the areas you are less proficient in, so that you can focus on your strengths.
3. **Value passion and teach-ability over experience.** When making their first hire, many business owners want to bring in an experienced employee who can hit the ground running. This is often a mistake, because it often leads the business owner to give up too much control of the operation to their new employee. It's only natural that you would let your experienced employee do things the way he or she has always done them, right. But if you are trying to differentiate yourself from your

competition, the last thing you want it to be just like everyone else. Instead, look for a passionate, dedicated employee who is willing to buy into YOUR system and wholeheartedly believes in your product or service.

Hiring your first employee is a huge decision. A good hire will kick-start the growth of your business, while a mistake could set you back months, or even years. Take the time to do it right!

5 WAYS TO BOOST TEAMWORK IN YOUR WORKPLACE

Even if your company is small, possibly only you and a partner, teamwork is the foundation of long-term success. So ask yourself this question: Do I support an environment that fosters teamwork?

Consider the three following statements when assessing your organization's teamwork health level.

Do you have employees acting independently when you have instructed them to work with others? Do you have a common goal that is being ignored for personal gain? And when an issue arises, do employees ask for assistance or do they tackle a problem on their own even if they risk doing harm to your bottom line?

Did you answer yes to any of the three aforementioned scenarios?

If you did, utilize these 5 tips to increase teamwork and boost your company's success.

1. Clarify roles within the team

Per usual communication is king. Make sure you clearly communicate to your employees or partners your expectations. Make their roles well-defined and outline their responsibilities within the team. Once they know what is expected of them hold them accountable.

2. Know your team

How can you define individual roles within a team if you don't know the members of the team? Well you can't. Become familiar with the strengths and weaknesses of each individual team member. Familiarity will enable you to choose the correct roles which leads to happy employees and satisfied workers tend to stray from the team environment less than ones who conversely are dissatisfied.

3. Leave no team members behind

Keep everyone in the loop of the decision making process, absolutely everyone. If an employee feels left out this individual will be more likely to break free from the team. This once again points back to the importance of open channels of communication. When you share important information with your team they will be more inclined to do the same with you.

4. Cross training

Provide your employees with the opportunity to learn their co-workers jobs. This will enable your employees to understand your organization from different points of view.

Additionally it will further the teamwork environment by giving workers a much-needed backup in case they need to call of work or take a vacation. Nothing builds trust like having someone step up when help is needed.

5. Provide consistent feedback
Whether it's constructive criticism or a well-deserved pat on the back, offer continual feedback. But keep this in mind, when building a healthy team environment really learn to focus on the positive rather than the negative. A team that celebrates success together will more likely stay together.

BUSINESS MANAGEMENT SECRETS: BUILD A WINNING TEAM

What is one thing that almost every successful business has in common?

A great product, a huge marketing budget, and a strong sales strategy are all popular answers to this question, and they are all important.

But if a business doesn't have a **productive team**, it is not going to reach its potential.

An innovative product is fantastic, but without a skilled team to manufacture and sell it, it's not going to matter. A large marketing budget is a fantastic tool to help grow a business, but without the people in place to get the message out, no amount of marketing can save a business. And you can have the greatest sales strategy in the history of the world, but without a team to execute it, it's going to flop. I've seen each of these scenarios play out many times over the years!

A productive team ensures that your business systems run the way they were designed. A well-trained team provides great customer service and keeps the day-to-day operations at your business moving smoothly. Without a strong team, you as the business owner are forced to spend all of your time babysitting, leaving you with no time to grow the business.

On the other hand, an effective and well-trained team is the most valuable asset you can have. If you can depend on your team to consistently execute the systems that you have created, the sky's the limit for your business. And that's no exaggeration!

We are going to take a closer look at the process of developing strong teams in the workplace. In the meantime, take some time to evaluate the effectiveness of your employees. Are they motivated? Are they effective with their time and with your resources? Can you trust them to do their jobs right, or do you have to babysit?

BUILD A WINNING TEAM: SET THE STANDARDS

There's a whole lot that goes into managing a team of employees. But sometimes, especially when you're busy, it's easy to overlook the obvious. And I can't tell you how many business owners I have worked with over the years who have overlooked a critical first step in creating effective teams: defining their expectations.

Many business owners admit that their employees don't have clearly defined roles and responsibilities. But this presents a major problem. How are your employees supposed to meet and exceed your expectations if they don't know specifically what they are to start with?

If you haven't already done it, it is important that you take the time to define the roles and responsibilities of each position within your organization. Far too many business owners expect their employees to "figure it out" by themselves, to work together in order to make sure all critical objectives are achieved. And while this sounds great in theory, the real world tells us that if responsibility isn't directly assigned, important tasks often go uncompleted. Assign specific responsibilities to each position in your business, and make sure that they are clearly communicated to each employee.

Next, make sure that your employees have both the resources and the knowledge needed to meet their responsibilities. This is where many business owners go off course, they assign responsibility, but fail to give their employees the resources to accomplish their goals. This is demoralizing for your employees and fatal to your organization. Don't simply assign responsibility, take the time to ensure that your employees are in position to meet your expectations.

Finally, help your employees to see the "big picture" - help them see how their job ties into the larger picture of your business, and how they interact with other members of your team. Help them to see the purpose behind their daily work. And help them to understand how their job impacts the efficiency of the team as a whole.

You can't just throw ten people in a room and expect them to figure out how to get the job done. As the boss, it is your job to assign each person a specific role and then to give them the resources they need to perform. This will make your team more productive and more effective than ever before.

BUILD A WINNING TEAM: PUT YOUR PEOPLE IN POSITION TO SUCCEED

Put your people in position to succeed.

It may sound easy and obvious, but I can't tell you how often business owners that I work with don't stay true to this principle.

Think about the game of football for a moment. For a team to be successful, a number of players with very different skills must work together. On offense, you need several players with overwhelming strength in order to block the defense. You need players with the ability to run with the ball effectively. You need a quarterback to lead the unit and to make decisions while distributing the football. Imagine if the coach of your hometown team placed one of his linemen at the quarterback. It's a ridiculous idea that would result in spectacular failure and yet, many businesses make exactly this mistake.

It's critical that you understand that each employee is unique. In order to maximize the value that each of your employees provides to your company, you must put them in a position to best use their unique skills and abilities. Don't try to fit a square peg into a round hole!

Keep this concept in mind when you're hiring. If you're looking for a specific position, you should have specific attributes in mind. One mistake that I see business owners make far too often is making a bad hire because they are impressed with a candidate's overall skills or personality, despite the fact that he or she doesn't possess the right skillset for the job. Remember that you're hiring for a specific job, and that you need a specific type of person in order to get the job done right.

As a business owner, you need your team to take your business where you want it to go. Putting your employees in positions that match up well with their skills will help them to feel happier and more fulfilled and it will allow you to maximize the value they provide to your business. You want your people to be productive, so give them a chance! Put your people in position to succeed.

BUILD A WINNING TEAM: DEVELOP YOUR WORKFORCE

So far, we've discussed the importance of clearly defining the responsibilities for each member of your team, and of ensuring that you assign the right people to the right positions. And while these steps will help you create an effective and productive team, that's only part of the battle. You must also *develop* your team, helping them grow individually and as a team.

How do you make this growth happen? By providing feedback, and by providing the training that each employee needs to improve.

It's important that you take the time to regularly provide feedback and further training to each of your employees. I highly recommend taking the time to review each employee's performance on a regular basis, not just once or twice per year. Why? Because otherwise, your employees are flying blind. By regularly assessing performance and pointing out areas that could use improvement, you are keeping each employee focused and on track. Yet many business owners don't provide feedback more than a few times per year... how about you?

Providing regular feedback is critical... but it's only half of the equation. It is not enough to tell your employees where they need to improve. If you expect to truly get the most out of each team member, you need to provide the training necessary to help them achieve their growth goals. This may mean sales training, it may mean attending management seminars, or it may mean communication workshops. Whatever the case may be, the point is that you need to give your employees the tools that they require in order to continue their development. Otherwise it's not going to happen!

Investing resources into the training of employees who already have the ability to get their job done may seem like a waste of money. But this is shortsighted thinking. The truth is that the productivity and the effectiveness of your team plays a *huge* role in determining the overall success of your business. Don't sell yourself short, help each member of your workforce to reach his or her full potential.

BUILD A WINNING TEAM: FOUR STEPS FOR MORE EFFECTIVE TEAMS

One of the more challenging tasks for a business owner is to mold a group of individuals into a cohesive and effective team. Effective teams are critical for business success, so here are four tips to help you create stronger teams in your workplace.

1. **Define expectations.** It's important that each member of your team has a clear understanding of your expectations - expectations for the team as a whole, and expectations for each member of the team. It's important that each individual has defined expectations, otherwise, individuals tend to relax and not take the job as seriously, because the whole team will have to answer for any failure. By holding each member accountable, you ensure that they'll stay engaged.

2. **Encourage communication.** Communication is critical, both between team members and with leadership. Maintain an 'open door' policy if you can—team members should feel like they can come to you with questions and concerns. Stress communication often, and make sure that team members are actively communicating with one another as much as possible.
3. **Provide support.** As the leader of a team, it is your job to make sure they have the tools they need to succeed. Whether that means providing smart phones, computing power or something else altogether, make sure that your team has the resources they need to excel. In addition to enabling them to do their best work, your support will send them the message that their work is important.
4. **Don't micromanage.** Nothing squelches ingenuity and creativity like micromanaging. Make sure that your team knows what is expected of them, that they have what they need to do their jobs well, and that they know they can ask you questions when they need your input. But resist the urge to meddle with the details of how they accomplish their tasks. Give them space to work and use their creativity, and you can be sure you'll get their best effort.

I've worked with hundreds of small businesses over the years, and I can tell you that strong teams almost always lead to business success. Are you getting the most out of your teams?

CHOOSE THE RIGHT GUY OR GAL: WHAT TO LOOK FOR WHEN HIRING A LEADER

Any time you hire a new employee, it's a big deal. You need to take your time and do your due diligence or you'll end up wasting time and money. This is exponentially more important when you're hiring a manager or somebody who will be in a position of leadership. While a great leader will get the best from his or her employees, a poor leader can ruin your entire operation. I've seen businesses set back months or even years as a consequence of placing the wrong people in leadership positions.

Today we cover several traits to look for when you're hiring a leader:

1. **Honesty.** This one is obvious, so let me just state that if you can't absolutely trust your managers and leaders, you're sunk. Make sure you examine each candidate's resume in depth—look for anything that doesn't seem right and investigate. Call all

references and specifically ask whether or not the candidate is trustworthy.
2. **The ability to inspire.** A good leader make people *want* to follow him or her. Leaders that inspire are priceless because they are certain to get the most out of their employees. If you leave an interview with a candidate feeling bored and unenthused, they're probably not the right hire.
3. **Vision.** A candidate may have all the personal qualities you're looking for, but if they aren't forward-thinking, what is the point? A good leader can evaluate the present situation, set appropriate goals, and figure out how to achieve them.
4. **Passion.** Your leaders need to be passionate about what they do. Let's face it, some days you just don't feel like coming to work. But you do, and you work hard and effectively because you are passionate about your business. The leaders of your company need to share this passion. Employees will feed off the emotions of their supervisors and if your leaders are not passionate about their jobs, you can't expect your employees to be.
5. **Excellent communication skills.** A candidate that meets every requirement on your checklist but can't communicate effectively should not be considered for leadership. You need to be able to clearly communicate with your leadership team and trust that they will clearly communicate with

their employees. This includes verbal and written communications.

Hiring leaders for your company is perhaps the most important decision you will make as a business owner. Make sure that you take your time and perform your due diligence before making any decisions. If you can't find somebody that meets the criteria listed above, keep looking!

ARE YOUR EMPLOYEES FULFILLED? (AND WHY IT MATTERS!)

Most of you had "regular" jobs before you started your own business, and I'd like you to take a moment and think back on those jobs. For many, the first job came in high school or in college, and was often something along the lines of working in fast food or in retail. Many of you also worked jobs within the same industry that your business now operates, often starting at an entry-level position and working your way up.

Thinking back on this experience, here's the question I'd like you to answer: could you tell the difference between employees who were showing up solely because they needed the paycheck and employees who were passionate about what they did? Of course you could!

Employees who are there just for the paycheck typically work just hard enough to avoid being fired. They often show up late, take longer breaks than they should, and do their best to leave early. They typically offer minimum customer service and aren't willing to pitch in when a teammate needs them.

On the other hand, employees who are passionate about their job don't need to be motivated. The come to work each day with a sense of purpose, and they are largely willing to do whatever it takes to achieve their goals.

As a business owner, obviously you want your employees to love their job. You want them to be self-motivated. You want them to be willing to work as a team. The key to achieving this goal is to make your workplace a place in which employees can find fulfillment. You need to give your employees a *reason* to come to work each day.

When I talk about fulfilling workplaces, many people immediately start thinking of charitable organizations and nonprofits. And while those types of operations *are* certainly fulfilling workplaces for many people, a business doesn't have to be philanthropic in nature in order to be fulfilling.

What is required is a defined and appealing mission, a central, unifying goal that your entire team can rally around. It doesn't have to be grandiose. Amazon.com sought to reshape the book-selling business. Chase Bank seeks to be the most convenient, customer oriented bank ever. The reason I and my team come to work each morning is because we are passionate about helping business owners grow their businesses and achieve freedom.

What's your company mission? Have you identified it? Have you articulated it to your employees? If not, you can't expect your team to come to work each day *excited* about what they are going to accomplish. So get busy!

Are your employees fulfilled?

HOW TO MANAGE PROJECTS MORE EFFECTIVELY: THREE STEPS

As a business owner, you wear many hats. And one of them is "Project Manager."

Whether it is overseeing production, running a strategic marketing campaign, or managing customer relationships, you typically spend a large portion of your day overseeing projects. (I know I do!)

Traditional project managers, such as managers in the construction industry, go through years of training in order to maximize quality and effectiveness. On the other hand, most business owners have no formal training in this area.

That's OK – most of you don't *need* formal training. But it is important that you continue to learn and refine your approach to produce the best results possible.

Below are three elements that should be in place *before* you launch any project. How well are you doing?

1. **Know where you're going... and why.** What is the purpose of your project? What are the final deliverables? What is the expected timeframe? It's important to communicate with all parties to ensure that everyone is on the same page. I've heard plenty of horror stories from business owners who have spent months working on a project of some type, only to discover that their customer had something else in mind. The wasted time and resources could have easily been avoided with better communication ahead of time.
2. **Plan before you act.** Take time to think the project through - are there multiple phases involved? Are there elements that cannot be started until other elements are completed? What areas demand priority? Create a master plan and assign your staff and your resources accordingly. This may sound obvious, but I can't tell you how many projects I have seen go wrong... just because they weren't planned thoroughly ahead of time!
3. **Set clear expectations for your team.** In step one, you've identified *what* you are going to do. In step two, you've identified *how* you are going to do it. Now, it's important that you *communicate* this information to your team. Who is responsible for specific action items? What are your deadlines? Take the time to communicate your expectations and urge your team to ask questions if there is anything they don't understand. I can't emphasize

enough how important this is. Just because *you* understand something doesn't mean that your team does. Don't take any chances - make SURE everyone is on the same page.

While there have been entire textbooks written on the topic of project management, these three steps will ensure that you start every project on the right foot. Put them into practice the next time you kick off a project!

WHAT CAN YOU DO WHEN TOUGH FEEDBACK UPSETS AN EMPLOYEE?

We have talked quite a bit about the importance of delivering feedback to your employees. Effective feedback is essential when it comes to developing top-notch employees and teams.

But that doesn't mean it's easy, and sometimes it can lead to employees with hurt feelings or bruised egos.

Several of my clients recently faced such a challenge, so today I thought that I would share my thoughts on the matter with you. Specifically, the question I was asked was "how can I get the employee 'back in the fold' after delivering tough but necessary feedback?"

I have four specific recommendations--- the first two which must be implemented during the feedback session.

Explain to your employee that you are sharing feedback specifically because you care about them and

want them to succeed. Critical feedback can often feel like a personal attack—so make it clear that your motivation is ultimately to help your employee become more skilled and more successful. Explain that if you didn't care about them, you wouldn't have brought the issue up to begin with.

End the conversation by focusing on the future. At the end of your conversation, put the past completely in the past. Discuss the path forward—what you expect from your employee, the benefits he or she can expect from doing so, and so on. It's important to end the meeting on a positive, optimistic, forward-looking note, as that minimizes the chances of your employee sulking and developing a negative mindset.

Acknowledge progress. After delivering your feedback, keep a close eye on the employee and look for opportunities to encourage him. It is important that your employee's hard work be recognized. It is never easy to break old habits and step outside of one's comfort zone—so be encouraging and let the employee know you appreciate his efforts.

Demonstrate your trust. Often, an employee who has just received tough feedback will feel like he's "in the doghouse." Prove that this isn't the case by giving the employee a new task, project, or responsibility whenever you have an opportunity. Don't just tell the employee that you appreciate their hard work and their dedication—back it up with actions!

Giving feedback is essential. But it really can upset your employees, so keep these steps in mind the next time you've got tough feedback to deliver.

EMPLOYEE EVALUATIONS CAN BE EXTREMELY VALUABLE... ARE YOURS?

Many business owners look at yearly employee evaluations as a chore that must be done and often as nothing more than the time to discuss a raise in pay.

I used to think the same way.

But that approach is wrong. In fact, employee evaluations represent a valuable opportunity to motivate and guide each member of your team as they seek to grow within your organization. Below are my suggestions to help you get the maximum value out of your employee evaluations.

1. **Do not make them an annual event.** The point of an evaluation is to give your employee feedback and encouragement as he or she grows into the role you have envisioned for them. So why the heck would you limit this to once per year? I recommend quarterly evaluations. (And "informal" feedback

sessions as frequently as possible.) This gives you the opportunity to both provide feedback / coaching and evaluate progress on a regular basis.
2. **Do not focus on the money.** Both employers and employees tend to view evaluations as nothing more than the time to discuss a raise. I recommend scheduling separate meetings… one to discuss your evaluation, and the other to talk about the money. Otherwise, your employees are going to be thinking about their raise the entire time and everything you share will go in one ear and out the other.
3. **Do not make evaluations all about you.** Yes, the primary purpose of your evaluation is to help each employee grow into a more valuable resource for your organization. But, you should also view an evaluation as an opportunity to help your employee grow into a more effective individual as well. Take the time to point out areas of potential improvement that may not directly impact the employee's performance at work. When your employees realize that you are genuinely interested in their development, and not just in ways that benefit your company, they will become that much more appreciative of you.

The opportunity to provide feedback and coaching to your employees is valuable, it is unfortunate that many business owners fail to take full advantage. Your employees are the backbone of your business, so take every opportunity to help them grow… both personally and professionally!

FOUR WAYS TO REDUCE EMPLOYEE TURNOVER

Looking to cut costs? Here's a less-obvious way to do so: reduce your employee turnover rate. It is estimated that the cost of replacing an employee is approximately one third of that employee's annual salary. In other words, if you're paying an employee $35,000 per year, it will cost you just under $12,000 to hire and train a replacement. Obviously the moral of that story for business owners is this: keeping employee turnover as low as possible can dramatically improve your bottom line. Keep reading for some suggestions on how to lower your turnover rate and keep it low:

1. **Hire carefully.** The best way to keep turnover low is to make each hiring decision carefully. Interview candidates thoroughly and try to hire candidates who you expect to be happy with your company for years to come. Be sure to do your due diligence—calling a candidate's previous employers is

often a helpful way to identify potential problems before it is too late.

2. **Keep employees engaged.** One of the top reasons that employees leave a job is that they feel unappreciated and unimportant. Do your best to keep each employee engaged. Seek their input from time to time and be sure to offer positive reinforcement often. Whether we admit it or not, the desire to be praised is present in all of us. By complementing your employees and making it clear that they are important, you are greatly reducing the chances that they'll decide to leave.

3. **Don't burn them out.** It's tempting to keep asking for more from your employees, especially the really good ones. But overworking them is a bad long-term decision. Even if they're not complaining, be very careful not to overload any employee. Surveys have shown that employees today desire a healthy balance of their work life and their personal life, and not allowing such a balance is a sure way to drive good employees out the door.

4. **Give them opportunities to grow.** Your best employees are driven and ambitious. That can actually pose a problem from a managerial standpoint if you don't recognize their drive. If an employee has mastered his or her current job, find them a new challenge. This doesn't have to mean moving them to a different department or rewriting their job description—simply adding more

responsibility can be enough to keep them happy and engaged. The bottom line is that your best employees expect to grow as time passes. They'll expect more responsibility, fresh challenge and higher compensation. Develop a long term plan to keep these employees happy and you can be sure they'll be with you for the long haul.

THREE WAYS TO KEEP YOUR EMPLOYEES ENGAGED

If your employees come to work each morning motivated solely by the need for their next paycheck, there's no way that you'll be receiving their best effort. We've discussed this before, and it's true: employees who are working solely for a paycheck typically do just enough to get by and to avoid negative attention. They don't generally go the extra mile, they don't employ their creative energies to find a solution for a tough problem, and they don't look for opportunities to innovate or provide additional value to customers.

On the other hand, an engaged and motivated workforce is an invaluable asset to your business. So how can you keep your employees engaged and productive? Here are three suggestions:

1. **Provide incentive.** Give your employees incentive to produce at a high level. Performance bonuses

are often thought of as the only way to do this, but there are plenty of other methods you can use. Reward high performing employees with additional responsibilities and opportunities. Make sure that employees understand that your standards are high—do not tolerate subpar work. When an employee does a great job make sure that they are publically acknowledged. It's human nature to desire praise and positive feedback, so provide it when employees deserve it.
2. **Develop teamwork.** A good team is more than the sum of its parts. When you create a strong team, your employees are more productive working together than they are by themselves. Each individual has strengths and weaknesses, and working as a team allows employees to focus on their strengths. In addition, the strong bonds that form between team members will provide additional motivation to get the job done right. This will take some effort from you at the outset. Team Building activities or even a night out as a group can be a great beginning.
3. **Empower employees.** You can't expect great things from employees if they don't have what they need to do a good job, so be sure they have both the tools and the confidence they need to succeed. Encourage creativity and allow them to make decisions without consulting you first. This will make them feel less like brainless robots and more like important members of your team. All of

us naturally desire a sense purpose, and by making it clear that you're depending on them, you'll be giving your employees a reason to wake up each morning excited to go to work.

SMALL, FOCUSED TEAMS CAN ACCOMPLISH BIG THINGS

Strong teams are much more than the sum of their parts. While individuals each have their unique strengths and weaknesses, working in teams allows the strengths of each individual to be leveraged and their weaknesses to be protected.

In my own businesses and in those of my clients, we've been able to accomplish big things by utilizing the power of teamwork. I've seen innovation take place at break-neck speed thanks to the combined brilliance of the team members. I've seen managers turn their departments around by changing the mindset from one of individualism to one of teamwork and cohesion. I've seen problems that have held businesses back *for years* overcome by focused teamwork.

Strong teams are the foundation of business success—I've seen this proven time and time again over the years.

But it is not enough to simply throw a group of people together and hand them an assignment.

For one thing, size matters. I have found that, both in my own businesses and in the businesses that my clients own, that teams of 3-6 people are typically far more effective than larger teams. This is the case for a number of reasons:

- Smaller teams mean more accountability. No team member can "blend into the shadows" on a small team.
- Smaller teams mean more efficiency. There is less time spent bickering and deciding on a course of action, but the benefits of multiple viewpoints and perspectives still apply.
- Smaller teams ensure contribution from every member. In groups of ten, twelve, or twenty, it's common for a few outspoken members to dominate the conversation and the decision-making process. Small teams ensure that introverts feel comfortable as well—and that they are able to add value.

Granted there are certain situations that call for more manpower, but in general smaller teams are the route to pursue.

Size is only an element of the question, however. If you want results from your teams, you need to empower them. That means:

- Don't paralyze them by requiring that you sign off on every single decision. If you trust your people, give them the autonomy they need to be effective. If you don't trust your people… that's a different conversation altogether!
- Provide the resources necessary. I'm not just talking about money, although that is often important. Without the time to collaborate, your teams can't be effective. Google famously required their engineers to spend 20% of their time (a full workday!) each week working on pet projects. Take the same approach with your teams.
- Require *results,* not paperwork. At the end of the day, what do you want from your team—paperwork, excuses, or results? Don't waste their time by requiring unnecessary paperwork, and make it clear that you aren't interested in excuses. Demand results—and reward teams that produce.

STOP MAKING LIFE DIFFICULT... START MAKING MORE MONEY!

"Keep it simple, stupid." Most of us are familiar with this concept.

But I've found something interesting as I've worked with clients over the years - many are creating unnecessary levels of complexity for themselves, their employees and their customers.

The result is that employees' jobs become more complicated. Managers have a more difficult time overseeing things. And the customer experience becomes less pleasant.

Below are three common ways that these situations are created:

1. **Failure to train properly.** Most owners and managers go to one extreme or the other when it comes to managing their employees—they either micromanage to the point of suffocation, or they

basically do nothing and leave the employee to fend for himself. We have talked a lot about the dangers of micromanagement—but too little management is equally bad. Rather than creating systems and procedures to simplify the jobs of their employees, many managers leave details completely up to their employees. As a result, there is no standardization, there are no universal procedures, and there is constant confusion as employees try to figure things out on the fly.

2. **Failure to communicate clearly with customers.** Is it easy for your customers to understand the goods and services you offer? Do they clearly understand the benefits you provide? Is your pricing easy to grasp? If not, you are asking them to work too hard - and they'll go elsewhere. You should be able to clearly explain the benefits you offer in a couple of sentences. If you can't, you need to simplify. That doesn't mean dumbing down your products or services… but it does mean you need to find a better way to communicate with your customers. Assume that your customer is coming to you with the perspective, *"Don't make me think!"*

3. **Unclear organizational structures.** Many small business owners have a poorly defined chain of command. Many employees don't know who their boss is, other than thinking the only boss is you. So you end up wasting time answering questions and solving problems that frankly aren't worth

your time to deal with. Everyone on your team should have clearly defined responsibilities and a defined supervisor. You'll be amazed how effectively your business will run once each employee knows exactly where they fit in the system.

Take a good hard look at your organization. Is there uncertainty and inefficiency that can be eliminated? Doing so will help you make more money, so it's an exercise worth pursuing!

BUILD STRONGER TEAMS: THREE STEPS FOR MAXIMUM EFFECTIVENESS

Most small businesses utilize teams in the workplace, formally or informally. Whether it is two employees collaborating in order to solve a customer's problem or a group of five tasked with redesigning a product line, teamwork plays a major role on a daily basis in many businesses.

Over my years in business, I've had the privilege of working with hundreds of business owners. I've met their employees, spent time in their offices, and watched their teams at work. And as I have told you before, I am often struck by the difference in effectiveness of teams in different organizations. Many of my clients have phenomenal teams that produce consistent results. Others have teams that are barely even functional.

The impact that top-notch teams can have on the profitability of your business can't be overstated. Similarly, the negative effect that underperforming teams have on morale, productivity, and ultimately profitability is substantial.

Today, I'm going to share three tips to help you create stronger teams. Each of them has been tried and tested in the real world, and, if properly implemented, will make a real difference in your workplace.

Define expectations and create accountability. Perhaps the biggest problem plaguing many teams is a lack of clear expectations and accountability. Each team member should know exactly what is expected, when it is expected by, and how it is to be done.

1. **Promote trust in team members.** If your team can't trust one another to do their job, everything falls apart. One way to create this trust is to encourage members to socialize with each other after work by holding monthly staff events. It's easier to trust someone when you have a personal bond with them. But by itself, this approach isn't enough. You also need to demand performance. If a team member is consistently "dropping the ball", he/she needs to be retrained or removed. If you force your team members to work with an individual who continues to fail at their job, they'll never develop the trust they need to be effective as a team.
2. **Encourage communication.** Whether it is communication with you or communication with each other, your teams must be open communicators if they are to be effective. Problems should be quickly brought to everyone's attention, and

solutions communicated just as quickly. Team members must quickly be made aware of changing expectations and requirements. A team that fails to communicate is not a team, it's simply a group of individuals.

Effective teams are one of the most important elements of world-class businesses. Put these three tips into practice and you'll see an improvement.

5 WAYS TO DERAIL YOUR EMPLOYEE EMPOWERMENT PLANS

You have big plans for your company and it's obvious you can't make your operation a smashing success on your own. It takes teamwork to get ahead and that, of course, means you need help.

Help from people putting forth a concerted effort to achieve the same goal, but if those people feel alienated and abandoned, their only goal will be strategizing their exit.

Are you empowering your employees? Or are you derailing your own success by sabotaging the very people you need to win?

Here are 5 ways you might be undermining your growth by keeping your employee's empowerment at a minimum.

1. You don't communicate
A company without communication is like a sailboat without a sail. Do you provide feedback to your employees? If

not, it's time you open up the channels of communication on a daily basis. Consider implementing a plan that fosters communication and makes your goals crystal clear to your employees. Reward ideas, and always let your employees know that you value their opinions.

2. You express distrust
Do you trust your employees? If you don't, why did you hire them in the first place? When you add someone to your team make sure they are absolutely perfect for the job and then allow them to perform. Hovering over them, micromanaging their every move, not only wastes your time, it hinders their growth as an employee. Without trust there is no empowerment.

3. You never delegate
Are you working 90 hours a week even though you have an office filled with employees? You may have a delegation issue. The concept of delegating duties usually comes down to point number two (above), you don't trust them. Or you have control issues. Regardless, you need to leverage your employees. Use them to get the job done and possibly save your sanity in one fell swoop.

4. You criticize but you avoid rewarding
If your employees go above and beyond the call of duty, do you reward their efforts? For some, criticizing comes easy but giving a pat on the back is very difficult. Constructive criticism and a system for rewarding

exceptional performance are equally as important. Provide your employees with measurable goals they can attain and then reward them with cash bonuses, gift cards or extra vacation time when they meet or exceed those objectives.

5. You never challenge your employees
An unchallenged employee is a bored, disengaged employee. Empower your workers by challenging them to venture outside of their comfort zones. For example: an employee who fears leading others should be placed in a leadership position even if for a short period of time. You never know that employee may go on to lead your company to record profits.

IT'S NOT ALL ABOUT THE MONEY: THE TRUTH ABOUT MOTIVATION

How can you motivate your employees? Most business owners would quickly reply with "money." And while money certainly plays a role, the truth is more complicated than that. Money will only take you so far. Beyond money, there are three components that must be present to truly get the best out of your employees: Autonomy, Mastery, and Purpose.

Autonomy simply refers to the ability to make decisions for yourself. Give your employees a task (or set of tasks) but grant them the freedom to accomplish the task as they see fit. Some companies have given their employees freedoms like working from home a few days a week or telecommuting. Others have implemented things like flex scheduling, allowing employees to leave the office for hours at a time and come back to work whenever they wish as long as their work is done. You don't need to grant every wish to your employees, but if you allow them more control over their own schedule and way of doing work, you are more likely to get their best work.

Mastery is another important component of motivation. Give your employees the chance to become a master at something, no matter how simple. The process of becoming an expert at *anything* is an exhilarating and motivating experience for all of us. People are driven to learn, even if they aren't paid to do so! Give your employees the chance to master a process or a task and watch their production soar.

Perhaps most importantly, each of us needs a **sense of purpose** in order to consistently perform at a high level. What reasons do you provide to your employees to come to work each day? A paycheck? If that's it, don't expect your employees to even come close to reaching their full potential. Your employees need a larger goal to shoot for. Apple is dedicated to improving the lives of their customers through technological innovation. Starbucks donates a portion of their profits each year to a variety of worldwide causes. As a result, their employees are working for more than a paycheck—they are truly having a positive impact on the world around them. What are your employees working for?

If you want to get the most from your employees, you need to do more than just pay them well. Provide autonomy whenever you can, the opportunity to master tasks and processes, and a cause for each employee to work towards—and you'll be well on the way to empowering your employees and maximizing their productivity.

WANT TO BOOST EMPLOYEE PERFORMANCE? GET OUT OF THEIR WAY!

If your goal as a business owner or manager is to stay personally involved in every single detail of every element of your business, you don't need to worry about building an exceptional team.

On the other hand, if creating a systemized business that can run profitably without your direct involvement every minute of the day, getting the most out of your employees is essential.

For me it's an easy choice. I went into business for myself because I wanted *freedom,* not a job that consumed me 24/7.

So what's the secret? Believe it or not… you need to **get out of the way!** Before you can develop exceptional employees, you first need to empower them to perform at a high level. And that won't happen when they're being micromanaged.

Empowered employees are more motivated and far more productive than those who feel no sense of personal pride or responsibility in their job. Empowering an employee means giving them a true sense of purpose, and a reason to work hard each day. Employees who have been empowered will give you everything they have—whereas un-empowered employees will typically do just enough to not get fired. How can you empower your employees? Below are three steps you can take.

1. **Trust your employees.** If you do not trust your team, they will never develop the confidence in themselves that is necessary for them to reach their potential. Make it clear that you have confidence in your employees—both in their ability to execute assignments and to think for themselves. Let them know that you would not have hired them if they didn't have the ability to think critically and make the right decisions.
2. **Don't overreact to failure.** This concept goes hand-in-hand with point number one. If you expect your employees to grow and to take ownership of their jobs, you have to allow them to fail. It's inevitable that an employee will make mistakes from time to time (my bet is you've made mistakes too, I know I have.) When they do, don't scream, don't shout, don't overreact. Instead, sit down with them and identify *where they went wrong*. Turn

the mistake into an opportunity for growth. Help them to avoid repeating their mistake.
3. **Clearly define their role.** For an employee, an unclear role is very frustrating. Set clear expectation for every employee - show them how they fit into the system that you are creating. Explain how they are to interact with customers and the rest of your team. Make it clear that you expect them to think for themselves and make decision when necessary and let them know that you have confidence in their ability to get the job done.

You can't grow your business without empowering your employees.

BOOSTING EMPLOYEE PERFORMANCE

We began to discuss how you can "get out of the way" of your employees and allow them to function at a high level. The ultimate goal, as you'll recall, is to build a business that can run without your constant involvement—giving you the freedom of owning a *business,* not just owning a *job*. And you can't do that without a highly capable, talented team.

Today we are going to examine three more key principles as you work towards this goal:

1. **Create guidelines and set standards.** It's your job to give your employees the tools they need to succeed. This means that you need to clearly define your organizational standards. What do you expect in terms of customer service? Organizational relationships? Work ethic? By setting them on the right course, you free your employees to engage their intellect and their creativity without the danger

that they will wind up going in the wrong direction. Think of this as establishing the "rules of the game" that your employees will play by.

2. **Delegate authority as necessary.** Don't force your employees to come to you for approval 30 times each day. If you trust your shipping manager enough to hire him for the position, you shouldn't need to inspect each shipment personally before it goes out. It is important that you keep reasonable organizational controls in place, but if you refuse to grant any authority to your employees, they are never going to step up and take ownership of their job.

3. **Provide regular feedback.** The danger of granting too much independence to your employees is that they will wander off course. That's why it's critical that you provide feedback regularly. I recommend having a brief conversation at least weekly and anytime a teachable moment arises. This conversation is not a time for you to say "you shouldn't have done that, you should have done this." It's an opportunity for you to explain the *reasoning* behind the decisions that should have been made. As the saying goes, if you teach a man to fish, he can feed himself for a lifetime. Try to catch them, and complement them, doing things right more often than you catch them doing things wrong.

It may be a cliché, but the truth is that your people are your most valuable asset. I've seen what exceptional employees can mean, both in my own businesses and in those of my clients. But exceptional teams don't appear out of thin air. It's up to *you* to develop them and it starts with empowering them.

WHAT CAN THE NFL TEACH YOU ABOUT YOUR BUSINESS?

The NFL kicked off again this month. Many of us are devoted football fans, but for business owners, the NFL provides more than just entertainment. In fact, there are many lessons that business owners and managers can learn by paying attention to the action each Sunday. Below are three of my favorites:

1. **For a team to be successful, each individual must do their job.** Bill Belichick, the coach of the New England Patriots, has a sign in his office that reads "do your job." He doesn't ask any more or any less from his players—just that they execute their assignments. These assignments vary dramatically from player to player - the offensive line is told to protect the quarterback, the receivers must get open downfield, and the quarterback must read the defense, make a decision, and throw

the ball. If ANY player on the field blows their assignment, the play is almost certain to be a failure. How effective is your team? Do your employees know their responsibilities? Do they focus on them like a laser - and can you trust them to execute no matter what?

2. **A focus on the details leads to long-term success.** NFL players and coaches realize that they are in for a long haul. From training camp to the Super Bowl, the season runs nearly six months. And while they plan for the long term (every team's goal is to win the Super Bowl, after all), they recognize that it is the details that make success possible. You will never hear a coach fantasizing about the Super Bowl in week two of the regular season - because they are focused on their next game. Do you understand the role that seemingly insignificant details play in determining the long term success of your business?

3. **You can't control everything.** NFL coaches and players know that, no matter how hard they prepare and play, sometimes things won't break their way. And rather than becoming upset or despondent after a loss, NFL teams get back to work, seek to learn from their mistakes, and move on to preparing for the next game. How do you respond to adversity? Does it throw you into a funk for a month, or do you bounce back the next day? Failure is inevitable -

the question isn't whether or not you will ever experience it, the question is how will you recover?

When you boil it down, the business world is very similar to the world of competitive team sports. As you're watching your favorite team, see if you can spot any additional principles that you can take from the game and apply to your business.

WHEN IS IT TIME TO CUT TIES WITH AN EMPLOYEE?

Dealing with a difficult employee is one of the more challenging aspects of running a business. It's a subject that many of my clients have struggled with over the years. Firing an employee should be considered a last resort, as it means that you've lost out on the investment you've made into training that employee, and it means you'll have to spend time and money training a replacement. Here are three steps to take before you consider firing a difficult employee:

1. **Define your expectations and let him know where he or she is falling short.** When you have an under-performing employee, the first thing to do is sit down and talk through the issues. Let him or her know that they aren't living up to expectations and ask if there is anything that you can do to help them meet your standards.

2. **Do your best to re-energize.** Often, employee performance begins to decrease because they've lost interest in their job. To turn this around, make an attempt to re-engage them. If they feel like their talents aren't being utilized in their current position, consider adjusting their job description to allow them to spend more time doing what they are best at.
3. **Keep a close eye on the problem.** Once an employee has begun to underperform, you need to monitor the situation closely. It's possible for one "bad apple" to sabotage the morale of an entire team, and this is something that you can't afford. Once you've spoken to the employee about their performance, you need to see clear improvement or you simply can't keep them around.

If you've done your best to turn around employee performance but have not succeeded, it's probably time to cut your losses. If you're not sure, ask yourself these questions:

1. **Does the employee respect you?** If not, it's time to let them go. You can turn around poor performance and you can resolve personal conflicts, but it's very difficult to make a disrespectful employee respectful.
2. **Does the employee care about the job?** If he or she does care, you can almost certainly find a way

to turn things around. But if not, there's nothing you can do besides cut ties. It's impossible to get through to somebody who just doesn't care.
3. **Does he or she have the resources needed to succeed?** If not, firing them will not solve your problems. Evaluate the work environment and decide if you need to make changes to ensure that your employee(s) can succeed.
4. **Do you trust the employee?** If you're not sure that an employee can be trusted, it's time to let them go. Trust is critical to building a winning team.

Over my years working with small business owners, I have found that about 80% of the time the cause of an employee problem actually rests with the manager: the manager hired the wrong person, didn't train them properly, didn't provide adequate direction, or didn't provide adequate resources. So, if you think you need to terminate an employee, make sure you've done everything you can to save the situation first. Hiring and training a new employee is an expensive and time-consuming task that you should avoid if possible!

HONESTY IS THE BEST POLICY, SO MAKE IT PART OF YOUR COMPANY CULTURE

Can you trust your employees? Can they trust you? Can they trust each other?

If you can truthfully answer each of those questions with a "yes", I'm willing to bet that you're going to be successful.

Trust is a critical component of every effective team and every organization, but it's rare in the world of business today. How can you create a culture of honesty in your business? Here are three ideas:

1. **Promote open communication- even when it's hard.** An honest culture is not necessarily peaceful and happy all of the time. Whether your employees are honest or not, they are still going to have problems with each other and with management from time to time. Encourage your employees to speak their minds, respectfully and constructively,

of course. When employees feel that their co-workers and their managers will listen to their opinions, honesty becomes second nature.
2. **Create alignment of your goals with the goals of your employees.** Dishonesty happens when employees and managers have different objectives. If your primary goal is to make lots of money every day, and your employees' primary goal is to get out of the office early, open and forthright communication simply will not happen. Articulate your goals, and give your employees reason to buy in to your mission. When you and your team are working for the same goals, honesty happens naturally.
3. **Set the example.** As usual, the onus is on you as the business owner to set the tone. By providing honest feedback to your team, and by communicating openly with them even if the news is bad, you will inspire them to do the same. On the other hand, if you are only honest when it suits your purposes, do not expect any more than that from your team.

Trust is a big deal. Teams that trust their leaders and trust each other are willing to take risks, willing to innovate, willing to try new things. If that trust doesn't exist, employees are more likely to cover their own butts than they are to think outside the box. When there's no trust in your organization, you're not as effective. That's the bottom line.

WORLD CLASS EMPLOYEE ENGAGEMENT THE RITZ CARLTON WAY

Just like a rudderless ship will never reach its destination, an organization with disengaged employees will do nothing more than run in circles before eventually running out of fuel. An employee that is truly engrossed and enthusiastic about their place of employment is as good as gold and no company acknowledges this very fact more than the world-famous Ritz Carlton. Take note from this luxury resort and hotel leader and you too will have employees that are ecstatic, eager and completely engaged.

- **Respect your employees and they will in turn respect your customers**

When one thinks of the Ritz Carlton world-class customer service immediately comes to mind. This unequaled service starts with a healthy employee/employer relationship. The Ritz Carlton refers to its employees as "Ladies" and "Gentleman" and describes them as "exceptional." Foster a positive relationship with your employees from the very beginning and they will show the same respect to your customers.

- **Align company and employee core values with communication**
The Ritz Carlton makes its standards very clear and so should you. Create succinct reference cards that your employees can review daily to remind them of your business' core values. Additionally, taking another page from the Ritz Carlton's playbook, start each day with a motivational meeting. Have employees share exceptional customer service stories that will inspire them to go even further the coming day. Employee excitement will lead to employee engagement.

- **Empower your employees**
The exceptional Ladies and Gentleman of the Ritz Carlton are empowered to create a unique and unforgettable customer service experience. You interviewed, hired and trained your employees so it's vital that you allow them enough wiggle room to make decisions on their own. Provide your employees with the proper tools, tangible and intangible, to provide your customers with truly remarkable service without unnecessary limitations. Trust your employees to make the right moves autonomously and they will reward your operation with quality work and unmatched loyalty.

The Ritz Carlton leads the way in employee engagement by showing their workers respect, communicating core values and empowering their dedicated 'Ladies and Gentlemen' to create a fabulous customer experience. Follow this industry giant's recipe for success and your company can also experience world-class employee engagement as well.

YOU SHOULDN'T HAVE TO, BUT YOU MUST: HOW TO DEAL WITH EMPLOYEES WHO DRESS POORLY (OR WORSE!)

When you started your business, what did you have in mind? Freedom? Adventure? A six-figure income?

I'm guessing all of the above. What you likely *didn't* imagine were the challenges that come along with managing people - some of them seem quite ridiculous. Over the years, I have seen a whole lot of scenarios that I could never have imagined, let alone pictured myself dealing with them. And I've helped clients through many of these challenges as well.

Including, from time to time, employees who dress poorly or display subpar personal hygiene.

Sloppy shirts, wrinkled pants, messy hair and the seeming inability to shower... you get the point!

As a manager, oftentimes the first question that pops into your mind is "should I say something?" It's an awkward situation – because naturally you don't want to be offensive to your employee. So here's what you need to know.

1. **The problem won't go away.** It would be great if these types of problems would resolve themselves... but they never do. If an employee shows up once looking like he just crawled out of bed, he's going to do so again. And again. It might not happen every day, but it will continue to happen. Don't kid yourself - these problems don't fix themselves.
2. **Don't overthink it.** While the situation is awkward, don't dwell on it. Whether it's poor hygiene or sloppy dress, treat the issue like any other problem. Explain to the employee what is expected and hold him or her accountable.
3. **In many cases, the employee is genuinely unaware of the problem.** It may be obvious to you, and to everyone else in the room, but many times the employee has no idea anything is wrong. Simply discuss the problem clearly and professionally - most of the time, that's all it takes!
4. **If the problem persists despite your intervention, you'll likely need to let the employee go.** It may seem silly to fire an employee over his inability to iron his pants, but such as issue is usually part of a larger problem. It shows a lack of discipline, a lack of self-respect, a disregard for co-workers, and a willingness to ignore your instructions. Part ways before the problem gets worse.

If you own a business for long enough, I promise you that you'll encounter this type of problem. Don't ignore the problem, because it will only get worse.

DON'T LET SKEPTICAL EMPLOYEES SABOTAGE INNOVATION IN YOUR WORKPLACE

Change isn't easy. And it's not usually fun. But in today's competitive and fast-paced business environment, change is essential if your business is to survive.

Don't believe me? When is the last time you drove to Blockbuster and rented a video? Or called your local travel agent to book a vacation?

Today, we're going to talk about one of the more difficult parts of any change initiative, and one that doesn't get as much attention as it should—the process of getting your employees to buy in.

Let's acknowledge reality: most employees don't like the idea of change. It's not comfortable for anyone. And while it's certainly understandable that your employees are skeptical of change, it's critical that you bring them on board. I've seen change initiatives fail for no other reason than that key employees didn't buy in.

Resistant employees are not only slow to adopt the changes themselves, but they often have a negative impact on those around them. Whether it is by making disparaging remarks or through a more passive form of resistance, one skeptical employee can often be enough to undermine the entire effort.

What can you do to overcome the objections of your employees and secure the buy-in of even the most resistant as you implement change?

1. **Start by pitching the positives, but don't ignore the negatives.** It is important that you explain the reasoning behind your changes, and that you point out the positive impact it will have. That said, if you refuse to acknowledge any of the drawbacks of the project, you will lose credibility with your skeptical employees. Acknowledge that your initiative may make things difficult for a short term, but explain that the positives outweigh the negatives.
2. **Address any objections, spoken or unspoken.** Discuss your plans with your employees and take their objections seriously. Let them know that you do care about their opinions. It is particularly important that you pay attention to body language and other subtleties that may indicate passive resistance. Passive resistance is often more damaging than outspoken resistance—so seek it out and address it.

3. **Commit for the long haul.** Despite your plans and your best efforts, change is never easy. You are going to face unforeseen obstacles, and depending on the magnitude of the change you are seeking to implement, you may face exceptionally large challenges. If you show any signs of regret, or of defeat, your team will spot them and will lose the will to press on.

Change is rarely fun, but is often necessary. Innovation is the only way to keep your business moving forwards year after year. And it won't happen without employee buy-in.

Management systems guru, W. Edwards Deming, once said, "It is not necessary to change. Survival is not mandatory."

CUT THE CRAP ALREADY! (WHY YOU SHOULD STOP ACCEPTING EXCUSES)

You can provide great products and services. You can provide great customer service. You can market your products brilliantly. But if you cannot consistently meet the needs of your clients, it will not matter. Your clients need to know that they can depend on you to get their job done.

If you are a retailer, your customers need to know that you will have the products they need every time they visit. "Most" of the time is not good enough—if customers and clients cannot depend on you to meet their needs, they will go elsewhere... regardless of how high your level of service may be. I have worked with plenty of business owners who have learned this the hard way for themselves!

So how can you ensure a high level of consistency? One important step you can take is to *eliminate excuses from your company culture.*

To keep your business running smoothly, it is important that everyone on your team executes their responsibilities properly. And to make that happen, your team must understand that excuses are unacceptable.

Great businesses find a way to get the job done, regardless of the obstacles they may face. Below are several ways to eliminate excuses from your company culture:

1. **Plan for contingencies.** The best way to eliminate excuses is to make sure that each employee has everything they need to get the job done. That may mean having spare parts on hand, or it may mean giving an employee longer than necessary to get a job done in order to allow for challenges that arise. Plan for things to go wrong, because sooner or later they will!

2. **Encourage innovation.** From time to time, unexpected obstacles appear. We've all been there! Emphasize the importance of creative problem solving. There is a solution for every problem—but it may take creativity and ingenuity to make it happen. Work with your employees to create a habit of innovation so that they're prepared when they run into a challenge.

3. **Lead by example.** Do whatever it takes to meet your own obligations. If that means staying late, coming in early, working through lunch, or whatever—show that you will not stop until the job is done right. Not only will employees understand that you are serious about meeting deadlines—they will naturally strive to follow your example

because they will be able to see the value you place on always getting the job done. On the flip side, if they see you making excuses, they are going to do the same!

Excuses can poison a great business. The bottom line is that your customers expect consistency from you—you need to deliver. Teach your employees to plan, innovate, and to get creative when necessary. Do not accept excuses—because your customers won't!

DELEGATION AND FOLLOW-UP: WILL THE JOB GET DONE?

Do you have confidence in your employees to handle their responsibilities and get their assignments done properly?

Many of the small business owners that I work with struggle with developing a team of employees that reliably get the job done. It may seem like an obvious point, but businesses and organizations that communicate effectively and whose employees handle their responsibilities and assignments properly are at a tremendous advantage to their competition. So be honest—how well does your organization communicate?

Think about a recent failure… a production mistake, a marketing disaster, or whatever the case may be. What went wrong? Most of the time, poor communication is to blame, as opposed to individual failure. In other words, it's much more likely that, somewhere in the chain of communication, the instructions were misunderstood or lost altogether than it is that any employee failed to carry out his or her responsibilities.

The key to keeping your business running smoothly is clear communication.

Every time instructions are given, an opportunity for misunderstanding occurs. If your instructions are relayed several times down the chain of command, there's a strong chance that something will get lost along the way. Peter Bregman of the Harvard Business Review, along with many other experts, suggests solving this problem by using some form of a checklist. Bregman recommends a "hand-off checklist" which should be used each time information and responsibility regarding a task or project is exchanged, featuring questions like:

- What do you understand the priorities to be?
- What concerns or ideas do you have that have not already been mentioned?
- What are your key next steps, and by when do you plan to accomplish them?

The goal is to ensure that each exchange of information is accurate. Obviously, each organization should develop their own version of the checklist to address their specific needs. It may seem like overkill, but think of the headaches you could avoid if miscommunication was no longer a problem.

Even if you don't adopt a checklist, the main point I want you to take away from this is that an effective workplace requires clear communication. Going the extra mile to make sure that your instructions are clear and that those responsible understand what you're expecting will save you time and frustration. It will enable you to delegate a task and feel confident that it will be done properly. At the end of the day, clear communications enable you to better serve your clients... and that's what we're all after.

DO YOU HAVE A "PEOPLE PLAN"?

Many business owners don't think much about their employees—at least, not beyond the immediate "is he or she doing the job effectively?" question. It's understandable, given how busy most business owners are. Trust me, I get it! But the failure to create a system for attracting, training, and retaining talent will hurt you over the long run. At a minimum, here is what you need to consider when it comes to your company's people plan:

1. **How will you attract talent?** It's not enough to hire the first people to walk through your door in search of a job. In order to build a world class business, you need a team of employees that are dedicated, intelligent, and willing to embrace your system and your company culture. Even when you aren't actively hiring, you should be keeping your eyes and ears open for good candidates. And when

you are ready to hire, make a concerted effort to interest top-caliber individuals.
2. **How will you train your talent?** Hiring talented employees is a great place to start, but if you simply throw them into the fire and expect them to figure things out on their own, you are going to be disappointed. Before making a hire, make sure that you have a detailed plan for training and mentoring each employee. Sit down with them on a regular basis and evaluate their process, and identify any areas in need of improvement. By continuing to train your employees, even after they have learned the basics, you will enable them to reach their full potential.
3. **How will you retain your talent?** Once you have invested into hiring and training great employees, nothing is more disappointing than watching them leave. Be proactive... do everything you can to keep your employees engaged and fulfilled. This includes offering a salary comparable to the competition, but it is much more than just money. Work to empower your employees, and to give them a purpose behind their work. When employees feel valued and truly believe in the cause they are working for, they are highly unlikely to walk away.

Attract, train, and retain. If you expect to build a successful business over the long term, it is essential that you create a detailed people plan for your business. Without the right people to execute the systems you create, your business is never going to reach its potential. On the other hand, a talented and committed workforce will take your company to places you never thought possible.

MANAGEMENT SECRETS: MAXIMIZE EMPLOYEE PRODUCTIVITY

Large corporations have entire departments dedicated to employee management, but I am guessing that most of your businesses don't have the resources to hire an HR manager, let alone an entire department.

And while it's great to run a streamlined operation, the reality is that managing people isn't easy. Many business owners don't possess all of the knowledge that they need to get the most out of their teams.

Over this and the next two articles, we are going to cover the basics of employee management.

One of the biggest problems for small businesses is ineffectiveness on the part of their employees. Technology has only made this problem worse - between surfing the web, poking around on Facebook, and playing with smart phones, your employees have plenty of easy opportunities to waste time.

What can you do to keep them focused and on task? Below are three ideas.

1. **Evaluate employees based upon results, not time spent.** Part of the problem with employee productivity is that many employees don't have a sense of urgency. They know that, as long as they show up on time each day and sit at their desk, they can count on receiving their paycheck every two weeks. Don't let this mentality seep into your workplace - demand *results* from your employees. Give them tasks, monitor their performance, and hold them accountable for results. This approach will result in a more productive mindset for your team.
2. **Break up the monotony by scheduling "pace-changes" throughout each week.** Many offices quickly adopt a daily routine. It often starts with a morning meeting, before giving way to individual or team-centered work. And while there is certainly nothing wrong with establishing a routine, it is easy for a routine to turn into a predictable and, frankly, boring workday. So look for opportunities to change things up - vary your meeting times, hold an office-wide lunch, or whatever it takes to keep each day feeling as fresh as possible.
3. **Publicly praise productive employees.** Whether they act like it or not, your employees want to please you. It's human nature - we're wired to

succeed, not to fail. Turn this into an advantage by deliberately complementing employees who are consistently productive. Not only will you encourage them to "keep it up", but you'll encourage their co-workers to follow suit.

Motivated employees are an invaluable asset to your business. Unmotivated employees are an anchor holding you back. As a manager, keeping your employees motivated is one of the most important tasks you have.

MANAGEMENT SECRETS: HOW TO BUILD EFFECTIVE TEAMS

I don't believe that there is any ONE secret to business success. There are a multitude of important factors, systems, and decisions that ultimately determine the success or failure of a business.

That said, it is exceptionally hard to create a successful business without creating cohesive and highly effective teams.

Not simply effective employees, but effective *teams*. A strong team is much more than the sum of its parts. But they don't just appear out of thin air... so below are steps to get you started:

1. **Create teams out of individuals that complement one another.** You maximize the value of a team by combining individuals with varying strengths. Think about football for a moment - your hometown team doesn't employ 50 guys that

can throw the ball well. They employ 2 or 3 of those guys, and they surround them with other players of varying skill sets. This is an obvious concept when we relate it to sports, but you would be amazed at how many business owners hire the same type of employee, over and over and over.

2. **Build a sense of camaraderie.** The biggest hurdle to get over when it comes to team building is getting your employees to prioritize the team over their individual desires. The only way to do this is to judge (and ultimately reward) individuals based on their contribution to the team, and by the success of the team. Sure, this doesn't always seem fair. Employees may complain about being punished for the failure of others in their team and they may be rewarded for the hard work of others in the team. But, at the end of the day, if you want to build effective teams, you need to evaluate individuals based on the success or failure of their team.

3. **Assign responsibility.** A common downfall of teams in the workplace is that they can often be a way for individuals to avoid accountability. To counteract this tendency, it is important to assign specific roles and responsibilities to individuals within a team. As we discussed in point two, it's important to evaluate team performance, but it's also critical that each employee be held accountable for their performance. Assign clear roles and

responsibilities, and you won't have to worry about your team slacking off.

Strong teams will help you take your business to the next level. Do your employees function as a cohesive unit?

MANAGEMENT SECRETS: HOW TO KEEP YOUR EMPLOYEES MOTIVATED

The fundamental challenge, when it comes to employee management, is simple: **Your employees don't care about your business nearly as much as you do.** I realize this may sound harsh, but it's the truth.

That's not to say they are lazy, or irresponsible, or anything negative. It's just reality - you have invested time, energy, and money into your business. Your business carries it with it your hopes for the future.

For your employees, on the other hand, your business represents a paycheck. Sure, they may like what they do, but it just isn't the same. It can't be the same. They don't own your business… you do.

However, that doesn't mean you have to resign yourself to employees who don't care. You just have to think outside the box in order to keep them fully engaged. Below are four strategies that I have personally used to great effect over the years:

1. **Reward achievement.** The simplest and most direct way to keep your employees working to their full potential is by rewarding excellence. This can be done in the form of pay raises or bonuses, but it doesn't have to be financial. Consider rewarding employees with more authority, more responsibility, and more independence. Praise them publicly for a job well done!
2. **Match employees with the work they are best suited to.** It's important that your employees feel fulfilled while working for you. Do your best to put your employees in positions that match their skill sets. Sticking an out going, relationship-oriented employee in a room by himself with a huge stack of paperwork all day long is going to leave him discouraged, not motivated.
3. **Create a sense of purpose.** Everyone craves significance, it's human nature. Help your employees see how their work fits into the bigger picture. At Apple, for instance, the company vision is grandiose, they want to change the world. What is your business about? How do your products or services improve the lives of your customers? Give your employees a reason to be passionate, beyond a paycheck!
4. **Invest into the lives of your employees.** Spend time helping your employees grow as people, not just as employees. Teaching them skills that will help them later in their career, or in their personal

life, shows them that you really care. They'll reward you with loyalty and with their best efforts!

It's not easy to keep your employees motivated. But it's essential. These four strategies will help.

LEAVING YOUR COMPANY IN GOOD HANDS: TRAITS OF GREAT MANAGERS

Even if you have the ability to do it all, that's not a recipe for long-term success. Finding the right people to run your company while you are busy with other details is paramount for growing your operation.

But locating the right talent to captain your enterprise can be a difficult task and one that is vitally important.

Don't fret though because if you use a precise blueprint in finding great managers, you'll practically put your company on success autopilot. Here are 5 traits all adept company leaders possess; use this list when hiring your management team and prepare to be impressed.

1. Managers need excellent communication skills
A great manager doesn't possess good communication skills they are blessed with excellent communication skills. Even if a candidate fits the bill perfectly in all other categories, do not ignore this trait. A great manager knows when

to talk and more importantly when to listen. Additionally, after hearing concerns or feedback, a skilled manager will act accordingly. Think back to the leaders you looked up to in the past, it's almost guaranteed they were great communicators.

2. Positive attitude
If a candidate seems to have a rain cloud following them around everywhere they go, don't even consider them for a management position. Only place positive people in leadership positions because quite frankly negativity can spread like a bad disease. When interviewing a candidate really pay attention to the way they answer questions, do they trend toward being upbeat or a major downer?

3. A belief in transparency
Honesty is not only the best policy, it's the only policy. A potential manager that oozes distrust needs to be shown the door immediately. Don't even waste your time. A management candidate should highlight their belief in transparency from the start. That means transparency when it comes to dealing with his superiors – namely you – and with his workers.

4. Creative thinking
Sometimes solving problems takes a little creative thinking. Managers who reach levels of excellence find new ways to deal with old problems. When you look for management candidates, scour their backgrounds for examples

of creative problem solving and follow that up with questions regarding those examples.

5. No job is beneath him

A great manager not only knows his job but he also understands the responsibilities of all who work underneath him. Taking that point further, he also knows how to, at minimum, competently complete all tasks. A leader who can't roll up his sleeves and get the job done with fellow teammates is not a good leader. Ask candidates to provide examples of when they had to help co-workers, especially in instances in which the job was seemingly, for lack of better words, beneath them.

THREE WAYS TO DEMORALIZE YOUR EMPLOYEES AND MAKE THEM LESS EFFECTIVE

Running a business is tough, and you're constantly juggling priorities. But, it's important to understand that *nothing* is more important that your employees. Engaged, effective employees build winning businesses. Demoralized, disengaged employees drag the business down.

Unfortunately, many small business owners don't give much thought to employee management, and as a result make mistakes that lead to an unhappy, unproductive workforce. Below are three of these common mistakes… are you guilty of any of them?

1. **Putting policies ahead of people.** When you have thousands of employees, it's usually necessary to implement rigid policies. Until then, you should take advantage of your smaller size and focus on relationships both with your customers and your employees.

If someone needs to leave early, take a vacation day, or spend a little extra time on things other than business, accommodate them as much as you can. Your employees are likely to repay your kindness by watching your back and putting in extra time when you need them to.

2. **Not providing proper training or instruction.** Your employees may be smart but they aren't mind-readers. Make sure you are clear in your instructions, that they understand what you are expecting, and that they have what they need to produce the desired results. Otherwise, you are setting your employees up to fail, and that's not good for you or for them.
3. **Underestimating the value of relationships among your employees.** Make your workplace a fun environment— encourage strong relationships between coworkers. Whether it's occasional after-work events or simply eating lunch together, everyone benefits when employees genuinely like each other. That doesn't mean that they all need to be best friends or that they should spend company time telling stories or being otherwise unproductive, but do your best to create a fun and pleasant environment.

You need to get the most out of your employees. But sometimes that means relaxing your grip on the reins just a bit and remaining flexible. Of course you need to draw the line somewhere... but remember, employees that enjoy coming to work each morning are going to be much more productive and effective.

SMALL BUSINESS MANAGEMENT SECRETS: KEEP IT FRESH!

A common complaint I hear from small business owners goes something like this: "David, I'm in a rut. The days are becoming monotonous, I've lost the will to improve my business, and I've stopped looking for opportunities to innovate."

It's a common challenge faced by professionals everywhere, whether they own their own business or work for another.

But the stakes are much higher for business owners. While a corporate employee only has his own job to worry about, it is difficult for a small business to survive when the owner isn't fully engaged.

One of the best ways to avoid this problem is to keep your day-to-day activities fresh. Everything in life becomes boring if you repeat it often enough—think about it. You may *love* your business and *love* your role as the leader, but if you're doing the same thing over and over, it's going to get old.

This concept is equally (perhaps even more-so) true of your employees. They're not likely to say it, but if each day is a mirror image of the previous day, they're going to become bored, unengaged, and ineffective.

So what can you do to keep things fresh, both for yourself and for your team? Below are three ideas:

1. **Change your office layout about every three months.** Sure, this entails a bit of work on your part. But even a simple reshuffling of desks and workspaces can make coming to work feel new and exciting again. Consider bringing in plants, hanging new pictures on the wall, and other aesthetic changes as well.
2. **Start your weekly meetings by playing a game.** Most businesses hold meetings on a weekly basis, if not more frequently and they can be quite boring. Spice the meetings up a bit by making the content a game-worth-playing. Can you or a fellow team member bring life to the problem with real life human stories? Could you make a team challenge to solve problems? Perhaps you could get out of the meeting room and go out into the company environment or possible even visit a customer site to discuss an important issue?
3. **Keep your team challenged.** When you can see that an employee has mastered his or her job, give them a new challenge. This can be a new responsibility or a special one-time project. The idea is

to keep your team on their toes and to keep them from growing complacent.

Monotony is a very real problem for small businesses - both for the owner, and for the team. These ideas will help you keep things fresh on a daily, weekly, and monthly basis… but by no means is this an exhaustive list. Be creative and never stop looking for new ways to keep things fresh at your workplace!

DO YOUR BUSINESS TEAMS DELIVER REPORTS... OR RESULTS?

Teams play a crucial role in most businesses. Whether it's a team assembled to make existing processes more efficient, to eliminate manufacturing defects, or to improve sales, cross-functional teams are a fixture in the workplace. Teams can be very effective, as they offer the opportunity to combine individual expertise to create a well-rounded skill set.

But there are drawbacks to using teams in your workplace. One of them is that, in many cases, individuals in a team feel no personal responsibility for the project. As a result, there is little urgency and little in the way of productivity. There will be plenty of talk, plenty of meetings, and plenty of progress reports... but little actual progress!

So, if you use teams in your business, ask yourself this: Are your teams producing reports... or results? When you assign a problem to a team, do they solve the problem? Or do they spend weeks going back and forth before creating a vague report on this matter that lacks any concrete solutions?

Below are a few ways to make your teams more productive and results oriented:

1. **Set clear expectations.** First things first. Let each team know that you're looking for results, not excuses and certainly not an endless parade of progress reports. Define the problem, make sure they clearly understand it, and tell them to solve it.
2. **Define roles.** Each team should have a defined leader. When you appoint a leader, he will feel personally responsible for the success of your team. In turn, the team leader will apply pressure on the members of the team. This allows you to avoid the inefficiency that occurs when nobody on the team feels any sense of responsibility. But it's not just about the leader - each member of the team should have specific duties that they are responsible for as well.
3. **Provide support.** Make sure that the team has the resources they need to succeed in solving the problem. That includes time, physical space to work, a reasonable budget and any other specific needs. Remember, you're not looking for recommendations and reports, you are looking for a solution. And your team isn't going to solve the

problem if they don't have the resources they need to succeed.

As the boss, you set the tone. What is the culture of your workplace? Do employees have a sense of urgency? If not, you need to create that urgency. Without it, your teams will spend hours producing lists of recommendations and solving nothing. Make sure each employee knows that you're not interested in reports... you're interested in results.

IMPROVE YOUR HIRING PROCESS BY ASKING THE RIGHT QUESTIONS

Hiring can make or break your business – it's that important.

Given the expense of replacing an employee, and the impact that a single employee can make on a small business, hiring the wrong applicant is a very expensive mistake. To minimize this possibility, it goes without saying that you should carefully examine the resume and track record of each applicant you're considering, including contacting his or her references and previous employers. But beyond the obvious fact-checking, conducting an effective interview can help you separate the good applicants from the mediocre. Below are three tips to ensure that you're getting the insight you need from an interview:

1. **Go beyond experience.** Experience can be misleading. The specific demands of your available position require specific skills. It's entirely possible

than an applicant with years of experience in your industry could be outperformed by a recent college graduate who happens to have the right specific skills for the position. So identify the characteristics that will lead to success in the position you're hiring for. Then, ask applicants to recount instances from their past in which they have utilized those specific skills. For instance, if you value creative thinking, you may ask an applicant for a customer service position to recount a situation in which he or she thought outside-the-box in order to satisfy an unhappy customer. Conversely, if you expect your employees to stick to your established procedures, ask about an instance in which the applicant was able to stick to a previous company's policy despite pressure to deviate from the rules.

2. **Identify their level of enthusiasm and commitment.** Why is the applicant seeking a job with your company? Are they simply looking for any job they can find, or is there something about your available position that they are attracted to? An employee who is genuinely interested in their job is infinitely more valuable than the employee whose commitment runs only as deep as securing their next paycheck. Ask them simply why they want the job… you'll get great insight from their answer.

3. **Get a preview of their performance.** There is nothing more discouraging than conducting a long search process, finally settling on somebody, and

then discovering within the first week that they can't get the job done. There are great people out there who simply do things differently than you do—so get a look at the way they do things. Give them a scenario, and ask them to talk you through their approach to solving the problem. Make sure they describe their organizational process, their approach to communication, and their response to unexpected challenges. By identifying as many of their tendencies as possible, you should be able to weed out applicants who may be well qualified but simply don't approach things the way that you need them to.

Hiring your next employee is a big deal. Make sure you take your time, conduct your due diligence, and learn as much as possible about each applicant before you make a decision.

DO YOU SEEK AGREEMENT... OR CONSENSUS?

What is the decision making process like in your organization? Do you seek honest evaluations from a variety of sources, or do you expect your team to generally agree with your opinions? It's become something of a cliché that leaders should avoid surrounding themselves with "yes men," but in my experience, many business owners make exactly that mistake.

What does a healthy decision making process look like? There are several traits that every effective process has in common:

1. **Multiple perspectives.** Not just multiple voices, multiple perspectives. It's important that you actively seek input from a variety of perspectives… if that means asking an employee from each department to help you make a decision, do it! The key point here is that individuals with different

experiences and different areas of expertise may see problems or opportunities that never would have occurred to you. Don't let their viewpoints go to waste.
2. **Common goals.** Just as important as seeking varied perspectives is ensuring that your decision making team embraces the goals and mission of your company as you do. If all participants aren't on the same page with regards to overall goals and objectives, their insights aren't going to be as valuable. Make sure that your goals and objectives are well articulated and understood by everyone.
3. **Honesty... even when the truth is unpopular.** This is the key point that you need to take away from this discussion. In a healthy decision making process, participants don't hesitate to share their insights and opinions, even if they may be unpopular with everyone else in the room. As the boss, you need to set the tone in this regard by ***welcoming*** input that challenges your thinking and your opinions. It's human nature to dislike criticism—but ask yourself this: would you rather have a flaw in your marketing plan pointed out in a meeting, or would you rather launch the plan and have it fail miserably? Having the flaw pointed out in the meeting may hurt your pride or even make you angry, but launching a flawed campaign will cost you real money. Do your best to ensure that all

potential problems are spotted during your planning meetings, not in the marketplace.

It's easy to get people to agree with you as the boss. Creating a diverse environment in which team members are encouraged to think critically and question your decisions takes work. But it's worth it. Creating real debate and encouraging disagreement during planning sessions will give you a much greater chance of spotting mistakes before it's too late, and it will allow you to take advantage of opportunities that otherwise would have gone unnoticed. Your goal shouldn't be to secure agreement... it should be to build a consensus.

BONUS TIP - THE ULTIMATE PURPOSE OF MANAGEMENT

What is the Ultimate Purpose of Management?

Management boils down to just a series of activities intended to achieve defined objectives.

Management, at the end of the day, however, requires an overall direction that doesn't necessarily have an apparent objective. It is up to the entrepreneur to guide the team on that path.

However, the entrepreneur cannot be around all the time. Heck, even the managers aren't always right on top of every situation, nor should they need to be.

This can be overcome by creating a management system and a system of values that end up guiding the entire direction the company takes. Through consistent management and hiring practices, the way objectives are achieved, and that path becomes ingrained in the company and almost natural to all within the company.

We call this the Company Culture.

Through proper and consistent management techniques, company culture can develop that encompasses the values and natural behaviors of the organization.

Company culture empowers people to make decisions at the moment, similar to how the entrepreneur would.

This culture, when done right, should embody the same values the entrepreneur holds for the company. This can vary from business to business, but these values tend to represent how the entrepreneur envisions their company and how the individuals in the company make decisions and how they function in the office.

The company's highest mission should define this culture, it should be visible in every element of the company. Anyone walking through should be able to see it whether it is on the sales floor or in the broom closet. It should show in the way your employees converse, and how managers speak, it should even reflect the customers.

The Ritz-Carlton demonstrates their value and their culture with the simple phrase, "We are ladies and Gentlemen serving Ladies and Gentlemen," a phrase that sums up and is reflected throughout their company in every hotel.

This culture develops out of the vision of the entrepreneur, and the entrepreneur needs to have an idea of what kind of culture they want to foster. This is the ultimate purpose of management that the entrepreneur must have in their mind at all times.

But fostering a culture takes a constant understanding of what is desired, and that ranges from entrepreneur to entrepreneur and industry to industry.

This constant effort can be painful, so it is essential for you as the entrepreneur to be mindful as to what the end culture you want to develop is as well as some management practices and techniques to help foster that culture.

This book has already given you a few strategies that can help develop a company culture, but perhaps the most critical way to create a company culture is to get your employees and managers actively engaged.

This also ensures that everyone involved buys into that company culture.

Employees and managers who are actively engaged with the company and what the company stands for will start to accept the culture the entrepreneur lays out organically.

This is done using three major tools, communication, protocols, and relational interactions.

- Communication

Communication is a defining part of the culture as a whole, so it should be no surprise that communication is imperative to company culture. So encouraging two-way communication between all individuals in the workplace is the first step to growing a company's culture.

This can be handled in a number of ways from whether or not there are cubicles or an open office environment too if the CEO or managers have an open door policy. The specifics should vary depending on the company, but determining those lines of communication and how they take place should be determined and made uniform across the company.

The next step is creating an environment which is best done with:

- Protocols

In sociology, protocols are customs and traditions. It is the way people act, what they wear, what they eat, and their laws that govern that. In the workplace, you can mandate some of this with company uniforms and behavior they have for example whether profanity is accepted in the office.

These protocols help shape the company's atmosphere, which might be very relaxed or more rigid. This will vary depending on the office, for instance, an IT company might be more relaxed than a law office, but the environment should set the tone of the work environment.

The final step is based on relationships and management, let's call it interactions.

- Relational Interactions

These interactions are between the customers, employees, managers, and the entrepreneur and how each group associates with the other and themselves. This includes how employees treat and view each other, such as are they working in close-knit teams to accomplish a goal or are they individualistic trying to scramble up the corporate later.

It also includes how managers manage; do they yell at employees, do employees fear them, or are they more like guides who can help lighten the path and encourage and foster a productive environment.

It even applies to how the entrepreneur treats everyone in between. Does he want a company that treats its employees as cogs in the machine that can be changed out when efficiency calls for it, or more like a part of a growing family to have a particular set of values and commitment to the company and its products?

All this even applies to customers and the customers to bring into your culture!

Marketing to a specific client to encourage them to use your business as well as

Fostering the right interactions helps develop the culture and ensuring the interactions and the way employees, customers, managers, and you the entrepreneur treat and view each other is in line with that culture is vital to developing the culture needed for your company.

Through communication, appropriate protocols, and appropriate interactions culture can be developed far better, and these are the areas to focus on improving and how best to change a company's culture.

Some action steps to do this are to first look at yourself, as the entrepreneur, and see what your values are.

- Write down these values, formulate a mantra and hiring strategy out of your values.
- Lead by example, if you want a company with an open door policy, keep your door open.

- Hire people who show interest in the values you uphold.
- Reinforce and praise employees and managers who demonstrate your values.
- Make the Culture visible
- Be consistent.

It all starts with you.

Management's primary purpose is, after all, to carry the vision of the company forward, and company culture the mechanism to fulfill that vision, your vision.

Creating an engaging culture will lead you to success!

MEET DAVID HILTON

David Hilton, MBA, M. Ed., DBA, started out working in his family's "mom & pop" business, and soon realized that the business wasn't fulfilling his dreams, yet he saw potential for growth in that business. Over the next thirty-five years and many struggles, he grew the company to a multi-location, multi-million-dollar business where he recruited, hired, and trained over 500 people.

As a business advisor and CEO coach he has helped more than 250 other business owners reach significant success in their businesses. More important than the financial wealth he has helped owners create is the freedom he has helped them gain to enjoy their lives apart from their business.

For additional information, please visit: http://strategicvisionbusiness.com/

www.ingramcontent.com/pod-product-compliance
Lightning Source LLC
Chambersburg PA
CBHW031426210526
45464CB00005B/2074